THE
DIAMOND LIL
HOMECOMING

THE
DIAMOND LIL
HOMECOMING

Colonel David J. Hastings MBE

Dedicated to the men and women of the
2nd Air Division USAAF

The Larks Press

Published by the Larks Press
Ordnance Farmhouse
Guist Bottom, Dereham
01328 829207
Larks.Press@btinternet.com
www.booksatlarkspress.co.uk

No part of this book, text or photographs,
may be reproduced in any way without permission
from the author and the publisher

Front cover photograph:
'Diamond Lil' escorted by the Jaguars of No 41 Squadron
arriving at Norwich
Courtesy Archant – Eastern Daily Press

British Library Cataloguing-in-Publication-Data
A catalogue record for this book is available
from the British Library

Printed and bound in Great Britain by
4edge Ltd, Hockley. www.4edge.co.uk

© David J. Hastings 2012
ISBN 978 1 904006 61 9

FOREWORD

By Air Marshall Sir John Kemball KCB CBE DL FRAeS

When I was a young boy, we heard a lot about the Royal Air Force, but in fact in our corner of Suffolk the only aircraft we actually saw were American. In particular the B-24 Liberators of the 486th Bombardment Group stationed at Sudbury, just down the road from where I lived.

This experience made me determined to fly and I was lucky enough to be accepted for pilot training during my National Service. However, I so enjoyed the life that I signed on and eventually was appointed to a permanent commission. After flying Vampires, Meteors, Hunters and Phantoms, I was given command of No.54 Squadron flying Jaguars at Coltishall. There I met David Hastings and it is not surprising that with such similar early experiences we became friends.

Thus, when I heard of the plan to fly a B-24 to the United Kingdom, I was thrilled at the prospect of seeing one again in the air and pleased to lend my full support. The help needed turned out to be rather more than I, or anyone, expected as you will see as the story unfolds. However, the project was in the end a great success and a tribute to the dedication of David and all the crew involved.

Sir Kemball

Tostock
2nd August 2011

CONTENTS

Foreword.. 5
Introduction..7
Chapter 1. How the Project Began.......................9
Chapter 2. The Detailed Planning......................12
Chapter 3. The Journey Begins...........................18
Chapter 4. Departure from Fort Worth..................24
Chapter 5. Into the Arctic................................. 29
Chapter 6. With the US Navy at Keflavik...............38
Chapter 7. The Atlantic Crossing........................46
Chapter 8. Arrival at Norwich............................53
Chapter 9. The Base Tribute Flights and the Tour...57
Chapter 10. The Final Flight Home.....................66
Chapter 11. A Pilot's Thoughts..........................69
Chapter 12. The Aftermath...............................70
Appendices..72

INTRODUCTION

In 1992 a fifty-year old B-24A Liberator bomber made the historic 4,500 mile flight across the Arctic and the Atlantic Ocean from Fort Worth in Texas to Norwich in England as part of the 50th Anniversary Celebrations of the arrival in Great Britain in 1942 of the 8th United States Army Air Force.

This is the story of that memorable journey that inspired thousands of people on both sides of the Atlantic, a special tribute to the 7,000 young American airmen of the 2nd Air Division USAAF who, flying from bases in Norfolk and North Suffolk, died fighting for our freedom.

For me this was a special link with history. As a young aviation-mad schoolboy I had admired the B-24 Liberator in 1943, first at Horsham St Faith, then at Rackheath (where I was thrown off the base by Colonel Shower) and finally at Hethel where the 389th Bomb Group was stationed. At school we heard that the dispersals at Hethel were right on the back lane, so I cycled out to see. Sure enough they were there, but all the Liberators were away on a mission. Pop Gantus, the Crew Chief, saw me standing by the hedge and invited me on to the dispersal. When the aircraft returned he suggested that I wait on the proper side of the hedge as he was sure his pilot would want to meet me. Then a large silver B-24, with the name 'Pugnacious Princess Pat' and a glamorous girl painted on the nose, taxied in. The crew got out and I could not believe it when Lt Al Dexter walked over and lifted me over the hedge saying, 'Young man I hear you want to see my aircraft'. So began a wonderful friendship between the crew and my family. I was 'adopted' by Lt Al Dexter, Pop Gantus and all the crew, spending every day I could in the summer holidays on the base. I learnt a large amount about the B-24, including how to start the engines, and saw them through their thirty-five missions. We lost touch after the war, but after frantic searching we were reunited in 1990.

I am afraid that I am no writer, but I hope you will enjoy this story from one of the 'Diamond Lil' crew, of our fun, enjoyment, excitement and tribulations on that epic and never-to-be-repeated journey. Can I also thank Air Marshall Sir John Kemball for so kindly agreeing to write the foreword as well as for his wonderful support for the entire project. Finally, can I thank my publisher, Susan Yaxley, for all her kindness, advice and encouragement.

David Hastings
Colonel Confederate Air Force
Salhouse, Norfolk, England

OUR SPONSORS

Air BP – Bernard Matthews plc – NorthWest Airlines – Norwich Sport Village & Hotel in Broadland – R.G.Carter Ltd – Willhire Group Ltd – DJ Associates – Pelham Homes (Norfolk) Ltd – Airport Ambassador Hotel – Hotel Norwich – Wesley Coe (Cambridge) Ltd – Norwich Airport – The Muckleburgh Collection – Hoseasons Holidays – Air UK Engineering – Taverham Nursery Centre – Eastern Stearman – Norfolk Vintage Pilots – Air UK – NatWest Bank – Eastern Counties Newspapers – The Memorial Trust of the 2nd Air Division

and

the many private individuals who have helped to make this flight possible.

The B-24A Liberator AM927 'Diamond Lil'.

Chapter 1

HOW THE PROJECT BEGAN

This story began in 1991 when I was serving as a Governor of the Memorial Trust that administers the unique 2nd Air Division USAAF Memorial Library in Norwich. The Trust was approached by the East Anglia Tourist Board to see if we were willing to help with the 1992 celebrations to mark the fiftieth anniversary of the arrival in Great Britain of the American 8th Army Air Force; we were delighted to be asked.

However, at the first meeting in London, which I attended with the late Squadron Leader Berry Savory of The Muckleburgh Collection at Weybourne, it became obvious that if we didn't get a B-24 Liberator bomber to the UK, the B-17 Flying Fortress would get all the credit. This was reported back to the Memorial Trust and the late Tom Eaton, Trust Chairman at that time, really began the whole project by telling me, as the only pilot Governor on the Trust, 'David, find a B-24 Liberator and bring it to Great Britain.' I tried to explain that this would be no easy task as there were only three B-24s left in the world and they were all in the United States, and one was so full of corrosion that I would not fly it across the Atlantic. However, Tom Eaton would not be moved, and as you do not argue with your Chairman, I made a start on the project.

We start with the Collings Foundation

We had seen that the Collings Foundation in the USA had just restored an ex-Indian Air Force B-24 Liberator, so I called Robert Collings. He seemed interested and suggested that I should fly over to discuss the idea in more detail, and the fun began. He said that he would want £100,000 to fly his Liberator to England, and I told him that we might be able to raise that amount. When I returned to Norfolk, we made announcements in the local papers and the Aviation press giving details of this exciting project and the response was tremendous. I managed to get the *Eastern Daily Press* to sponsor us with full coverage as well as BBC Radio Norfolk and many local firms including Bernard Matthews, The Muckleburgh Collection, Norwich Sport Village,

R.G.Carter Ltd, Hoseasons Holidays, Pelham Homes, DJ Associates, Air UK Engineering, Wesley Coe, Taverham Nurseries, Norfolk Vintage Pilots and the NatWest Bank. (See full list of sponsors on p.8) We were also deeply moved by the many individuals, both young and old, who agreed to sponsor the flight. I needed also to get an airline on board to help with crew changes etc. and first tried British Airways. To my surprise they turned us down, as did Virgin Atlantic and the American airline, Delta. So I phoned NorthWest Airlines and here we struck gold. I spoke to their European manager, Bill Samuels, and he suggested that I meet him at their headquarters at Gatwick. Bill was enthusiastic right from our first meeting and we can never thank him enough. He offered us all our crew changes and promotion in both the UK and the USA as well as financial support.

Next was the fuel, a huge part of our costs, and I was again lucky as my first contact at BP felt strongly about this tribute to the Liberator crews and they kindly agreed to supply all the fuel for the Atlantic crossing. Then it was on to the Civil Aviation Authority (CAA) and the airports we would use during the six-week tour, and the various air show organisers. Everyone was keen and helpful; I think they all realised the great PR benefits of having a B-24 Liberator flying in the UK once more.

Support from the Royal Air Force

Finally we needed support from the Royal Air Force. As luck would have it, Air Vice Marshal Sir John Kemball, whom we first became friends with during his tour at RAF Coltishall, and who gave me my first flight in the Jaguar, was the Deputy Commander-in-Chief of RAF Strike Command. I asked him for four things: a Nimrod escort over the Atlantic, a meeting with the Red Arrows and a Spitfire, and finally an escort of Jaguars into Norfolk on our arrival to re-live the famous painting by William S. Phillips in the mess at RAF Coltishall entitled 'Welcome Home Yank'. Sir John Kemball was tremendous and gave us all four and, as you will see later, he saved the entire project when we got into difficulties over the Arctic. By now we had raised over £90,000, so Robert Collings flew over to see me and we signed the contract. The Trust, the Tourist Board and the 2nd Air Division Association in the

United States were all overjoyed and the dream of getting a B-24 Liberator back to Britain in 1992 seemed to be coming true.

Disaster Strikes

Then early in December 1991 I had a call from Robert Collings in the USA to say that they had started on the flight planning and having looked at the Arctic and Atlantic crossings they had decided to cancel. I was appalled, but could not persuade him to change his mind despite my reminder of the debt we owed to those 7,000 2nd Air Division airmen who lost their lives. I just could not understand their sudden change of heart at this late stage. They must have realised from the start that flying to the UK was going to be a challenge.

The 2nd Air Division Association was heart-broken, as were the Trust Governors in Norwich and all our sponsors. Having put so much into the project and raised the funds needed, we just could not abandon it now. I decided to telephone the Confederate Air Force at Harlingen in Texas as I knew from a previous visit in 1981 that they had a B-24 Liberator. They told me to contact Col. Al Stricklin at the Meacham Field in Fort Worth, Texas, where their B-24A Liberator, 'Diamond Lil', was based. I spoke to Al Stricklin and Ray Krottinger and explained what had happened and how disappointed we all were on both sides of the Atlantic. We all felt it was essential that a tribute should be paid to the B-24 Liberator crews in the 50th anniversary year. After a long and expensive chat they agreed to discuss the project and said they would call me back within a few days.

The Confederate Air Force saves the day

The call came, and with it the wonderful news that they agreed that the tribute must be made and they would bring their Liberator to England, but on one condition – and it was here that I got lucky. 'Diamond Lil' was a basic B-24A and needed four pilots for the transatlantic flight, but they only had three. If I would fly out to Fort Worth and convert on to the B-24, then they would come. I had no hesitation in accepting, though my wife Jean thought I was mad at sixty-one years of age to fly in a fifty-year-old wartime bomber across the Atlantic.

So we began to plan again with almost daily calls to Col. Al Stricklin in his office at Meacham Field. He was delighted that we had raised nearly £100,000 in sponsorship, that BP had agreed to supply the fuel and NorthWest Airlines were also on board. I was told that I would have to become a Colonel in the Confederate (since renamed Commemorative) Air Force in order to fly the aircraft, something I had dreamed about for ages.

Chapter 2

THE DETAILED PLANNING

Now we had to start the actual planning and I began to realise just what was involved in arranging a 4,500 mile flight across the Arctic and the Atlantic for a famous and very valuable historic aeroplane. First we agreed the crew: Colonels David Hughes (Senior Commander), Ray Krottinger (Commander), Al Stricklin (Pilot/Navigator), David Hastings (UK Co-pilot), David Kjell (Senior Flight Engineer), Henry Brand (Flight Engineer), Sam Mangrum (Flight Engineer), Starr Stone (Scanner) and Kathy Martin (Scanner). We would also have two passengers who were sponsors. In addition the CAF was offered full TV coverage by either ITV or BBC Television and made a decision, that we would regret later, to choose the BBC. This meant we had a television crew plus presenter, Simon Bates – a very full aircraft. Next was the actual route to be flown. We promised the 2nd Air Division USAAF Association that we would use one of their wartime ferry routes and for some reason David Hughes, a Senior Delta Airlines captain, chose the most northerly one via Frobisher Bay in the Arctic Circle, Iceland, Kinloss, Prestwick and Norwich.

With the route sorted, the night-stops had to be planned with hotel accommodation and fuel requirements covered. We planned to depart from Meacham Field at Fort Worth on Monday June 1st for the four-

The crew flight-planning at Fort Worth for the Arctic and Atlantic crossing.

hour flight to Minneapolis/St Paul International Airport, the home of our sponsors NorthWest Airlines. The next day we would fly into the Arctic for the nine-hour flight to Iqaluit in Frobisher Bay, our second night-stop. Next we would leave for Iceland and the NATO base at Keflavik; this was a nine-and-a-half-hour flight over the Davis Strait, the mountains of Greenland, the Arctic icecap and the Denmark Strait, finally landing at Keflavik for two nights with the US Navy. All being well, we would depart from Keflavik on Friday June 5th for the five-hour Transatlantic crossing to RAF Kinloss in Scotland for customs clearance before the flight to Prestwick. Here we would spend two nights to take part in their air show and formate up with the Red Arrows and the Spitfire as arranged by the Air Vice Marshal. On Monday June 8th we would fly the final three-hour leg to Norwich International Airport and the end of the journey. At all stops we had to ensure that fuel and oil were available and accommodation for the crew and BBC team, with costs agreed.

Next there were discussions with the FAA, the CAA and the Military about the routes and heights to be flown, our call-sign and the

Copy of the original Jeppeson Trans-Atlantic Plotting chart used by the crew for the crossing.

authorisation and collection of all the charts and airport approach plates required. The survival equipment and warm clothing was then listed as as well as the crew equipment and in-flight meals. Back at Meacham Field the B-24 'Diamond Lil' was undergoing a very thorough overhaul to ensure that she was on top line for the long haul; changes were made to make certain that all the engines and propellers had low hours, a massive task for the CAF crew.

Support in the UK
In England we discussed with Air Vice Marshal Sir John Kemball our need for a Nimrod escort over the Atlantic. He kindly allocated the task to No.120 squadron at RAF Kinloss. I was given Flt Lt Steve Rennison as my liaison officer; he was brilliant, as was Wing Commander Mitch Lees, the Squadron boss. They phoned to say how delighted they were to be given the task and looked forward to meeting us at the Keflavik NATO base in Iceland. Two days later they came back with some amazing news from their Squadron historian. Our Liberator AM927 was the eighteenth built out of a total of over eighteen thousand, and was originally sold to the French Air Force. However, after the fall of France she was re-allocated to 120 Squadron but suffered a landing accident on her delivery flight. She was returned to the factory and converted to a transport version, in which she served for the rest of the war. If she had not had the accident she would have fought with 120 squadron in the Battle of the Atlantic. Indeed her sister ship, AM929, did fly with the squadron under the command of Squadron Leader Bullock and held the record for U-boat kills. The squadron members were delighted that we were bringing *'their aircraft'* home. Even later, at one of our Norfolk film evenings, we found the co-pilot of Squadron Leader Bullock – a small world indeed.

Next came the planning for the six-week stay at Norwich. Norwich Sport Village in Broadland came up as sponsors for the accommodation and another local firm came up with the crew bus. Then we had to liaise with the various air show committees that were keen to have us attend: Prestwick, Boscombe Down, Cosford and Swanton Morley, Dunkeswell, Biggin Hill, Duxford, Woodford, North Weald and Birmingham, all requiring crew accommodation, fuel and oil – the list seemed endless. We also had to deal with the media, the local and national press as well as *Aircraft Illustrated, FlyPast, Air Pictorial* and *Aeroplane Monthly*, plus the *Kinloss Focus* magazine. We wanted full TV and radio coverage of our arrival at Norwich with the escort into Norfolk by the Jaguars from RAF Coltishall. We also planned a photo link-up with the Red Arrows and the Spitfire at Prestwick. RAF Kinloss also wanted a special fly-past to feature our arrival, so life was indeed hectic.

We then had to deal with all our sponsors and the many individuals who wanted a flight in 'Diamond Lil'. Obviously we were not allowed to sell flights, but it was agreed that some of our sponsors could be offered a free flight during the stay at Norwich. Then we had to start on all the printing requirements for the tour: leaflets, programmes, 'Welcome on Board' brochures, name tags etc. Our small team at D.J. Associates were kept busy. We had more talks with Group Captain Phil Dacre, the Station Commander at RAF Coltishall; they were delighted to be part of this exciting programme and planned a great welcome to join up with 'Diamond Lil' as we flew over Lincolnshire on our way into Norwich. We could not have asked for better support.

A Wonderful Link with the Past

Then came an amazing phone call from Bill Samuels, the European manager for NorthWest Airlines. Someone had told him about my wartime friendship with Lt Al Dexter who lived in Minneapolis/St Paul and flew the B-24 Liberator 'Pugnacious Princess Pat' (named after his wife) with the 389th Bomb Group out of Hethel. We had at last re-established our friendship in 1990. 'What would you think,' he asked, 'if we flew Al Dexter and his wife Pat over to the UK so you could both fly a B-24 once again?' I was speechless, and even more so when he went on to say that *I* would have to tell them. I telephoned Al to give him the good news and suddenly Pat took over the phone to ask what I had said to Al as he was now in tears. When I explained, she could not believe that they would be coming to England and staying with us. For all of us it was a dream come true. For us to have the chance of flying together in a B-24 Liberator once more and go back to Hethel and see Norfolk was just unbelievable.

Together again in a B-24. Lt Al Dexter and the author.
Courtesy Saga Magazine

We arranged for the USAF to fly a spare engine and set of tyres over to Mildenhall from Fort Worth to act as back-ups during the UK tour and Squadron Leader Berry Savory from Muckleburgh kindly offered to work with my wife, Jean, while I was away on the Atlantic crossing, to help with all the administration – what a true friend he was.

Finally all our sponsors who had been invited to fly with us had to be notified of their flight details. We had promised the 2nd Air Division USAAF Association that during our stay at Norwich we would overfly each of their fourteen bases as well as the Headquarters at Ketteringham Hall and the main USAAF 231st wartime hospital at Morley Hall (now Wymondham College). As navigator I planned to do this in five separate flights with three bases on each flight; this was when we would fly our sponsors. As it turned out the response to the flights was tremendous and we were inundated with requests to do them again. Bless the B-29/B-24 squadron of the Confederate Air Force, for without any hesitation, despite the huge cost of the fuel, they agreed to repeat the flights – as long as I navigated. (See p.56 for the tour map.)

We also had a wonderful phone call from the Norwich Airport Aviation Group offering to look after 'Diamond Lil' during her stay in Norwich.

Chapter 3

THE JOURNEY BEGINS

The departure date from Fort Worth was now fixed as Monday June 1st and so in the last week in May we were hard at work in Norwich finalising the plans and confirming our routing with Air Traffic. The first night stop was to be at Minneapolis/St Paul to thank NorthWest Airlines, then our next stop would be at Iqaluit in Frobisher Bay, followed by Keflavik in Iceland. On to RAF Kinloss for customs clearance and to thank 120 Squadron before going on to Prestwick for two days and for their air show. We would arrive at Norwich Airport in the late afternoon of Monday June 8th.

NorthWest had kindly agreed to fly me out to Dallas Fort Worth, and so on May 26th I caught the train from Norwich, complete with my small flight bag, widescreen camera and the videocam. At Victoria station I met up with my good friend Group Captain George Keith, ex-Station Commander at RAF Neatishead, now working in the MOD and living in Chorley where he had offered to put me up for the night. I had a great evening with him and his charming wife, Anne, both eager to hear about the historic flight that I was about to undertake. After an early breakfast the next day, George delivered me to the South Terminal at Gatwick and I checked in with NorthWest Airlines for Flight 47 to Minneapolis/St Paul. Here I had a wonderful surprise as Bill Samuels was there to greet me and had arranged for me to travel first class, so I enjoyed the VIP lounge prior to departure – everyone seemed to know about 'Diamond Lil'. Once on board the Boeing 747 the lady Purser got me settled into the luxury cabin with a glass of champagne, the Captain came to say hullo and on time we departed from runway O8R. A truly memorable lunch with wine was served high over the Atlantic and later on I looked down at the mountains of

Greenland from 37,000ft and wondered what it would be like when we returned home over those same mountains, but this time at 11,000ft.

At 1530hrs local we landed at Minneapolis/St Paul and there to greet me were Al and Pat Dexter, with Jane from NorthWest there to see that everything was perfect and so the links with history began.

The NorthWest VIP suite at Minneapolis. Lt Al Dexter, Pat Dexter and Jane (NorthWest PR Executive).

All too soon it was time to leave on the NorthWest DC9 Flight 407 to Dallas Fort Worth and on the descent I had a minor ear problem. Waiting at Dallas were Geoff and Terry Gregory, our long-time friends from the 2nd Air Division USAAF Association, as well as members of the Confederate Air Force, and I was soon on my way to Gregory's house in Garland. I mentioned the earache I had on the descent and he immediately arranged for me to see a great Dutch surgeon in their hospital, as this needed to be sorted out before I started the flight home. The surgeon was extremely kind, cleared the problem, and when I came to pay the bill told me there was nothing to pay as he never charged 'people from the Old Country'. He suggested that I get it checked again when I returned home, which was another story. A very curt Indian doctor at the Norfolk and Norwich Hospital dismissed the American surgeon's findings and said he was only after my money. He was speechless when I told him that I had paid nothing.

Conversion on to the B-24 Liberator

The next day Geoff and Terry delivered me to Meacham Field at Fort Worth to meet up with all my fellow crew members. They had expected a youngster and were surprised to find that I was in fact the oldest in the crew. I also found out that all the others were qualified both as pilots and engineers, which left me as a mere pilot, a situation that would be interesting when we did the engine change in Iceland. I also met the two girl Colonels, Starr and Kathy, who were to act as Scanners (observers) and they were super. Finally I was taken out to see the old girl herself, 'Diamond Lil' and she looked wonderful. I could not believe that shortly I would be flying her, indeed if you had told me in 1942 that I would be a pilot and help to fly a B-24 Liberator across the Atlantic I would have laughed at you. Now the work on my conversion to type began, and in Ray Krottinger I had a great friend who made the task both easy and enjoyable. The Liberator was very like the ones I had known in the war and the starting procedures brought back many happy memories of 'Pop' Gantus. One big difference was that bomb bay had been floored over so the narrow walk-way had gone and instead we had massive storage bins on each side. Back aft you could still see the marks in the fuselage where the top turret had been and instead of the waist gun positions we had canvas metal-framed seats running along each side and right aft in the tail was a small toilet.

Seating area back aft of the bomb bay where we rested when not working.

One happy author after completing his conversion.

The Confederate Air Force crew, led by Colonel Ray Krottinger, soon had this old English pilot settled in; I could not believe that I was actually going to fly a real B-24 Liberator as a co-pilot all the way to England. The CAF had checked us all into a very comfortable Motel on the airfield and our first supper together as a crew was a riotous one with plenty of Margaritas. I was formally commissioned as a Colonel in the Confederate Air Force, another milestone for me in this unique journey. The evening included being forced to ride a 'bucking bronco'.

On the Saturday we had to exhibit the aircraft at a National Guard Open Day at Meacham Field, so we taxied her up to the display line from our hangar with Geoff and Terry on board. It was the first time in over forty years that Geoff had been in a B-24 and the memories came flooding back as he stood in the open cockpit roof hatch just enjoying the sound of the four Pratt & Whitneys. Parked at the display, proudly sporting the Stars and Stripes and the Union Jack, we were inundated with visitors all wanting to know about our forthcoming long-haul flight and collect our autographs. They were amazed that we were taking this fifty-year-old aeroplane all the way across the Arctic and the Atlantic. Meanwhile the engineers completed their checks. In the early evening we taxied 'Diamond Lil' back to her hangar, tidied her up and then enjoyed another memorable supper with more of the traditional Margaritas. I was certainly learning fast what it was like to be a Colonel in the famous Confederate Air Force.

The next day we completed our full crew briefing, signed all the aircraft photographs to be given out in England and checked the quantities of PX supplies that would be needed for sale at the air shows. Also, in the bomb bay, we carried an almost complete spare engine. In the afternoon we carried out a thorough check on 'Diamond Lil' under the very watchful eye of the Squadron Commander, before giving the aircraft a final clean and polish so that she was all ready for the great adventure.

A final great crew supper (but no Margaritas) with Geoff and Terry Gregory and Jordan Uttal from the 2nd Air Division Association, when they gave us details of the great send-off planned for the next day – and so to bed. The journey of a lifetime was about to begin.

'Diamond Lil' outside Staci's hangar at Meacham Field after her pre-flight checks.

Pulling the propellers through at Fort Worth prior to departure for the UK.

Chapter 4

DEPARTURE FROM FORT WORTH

All the crew were up early for a good breakfast in our smart flight overalls and caps before we made our way out to a very misty airfield at Meacham Field. 'Diamond Lil' had already been pulled out of her hangar and looked superb. We loaded all our kit and met up with our two passengers and the BBC Television crew with Simon Bates. Then we started on the very thorough pre-flight checks followed by a whole series of radio and television interviews. The Heritage League of the 2nd Air Division Association then gave us a splendid 'Scroll of Greeting' for the 1st Taverham Scout Group who had asked us to build this 'Bridge of Friendship across the Atlantic' as they were due to visit the USA that month. We were all deeply moved to see so many 2nd Air Division veterans arrive to see us off. Geoff Gregory summed it up when he said, 'Have a great flight and I wish I was coming with you.' David Hughes, as our Captain, then gathered the crew together at the nose of 'Diamond Lil' for a final picture and television interview before saying, 'Why are we still here? Let's get going.' So we clambered on board.

The author receiving the Heritage League Scroll for the 1st Taverham Scout Group.

All four engines started and we came off the chocks at 1130hrs. The applause from the Liberator veterans brought tears to our eyes as we taxied away to the threshold of runway 16 on a typically 'foggy English morning' and we realised then what this historic flight was all about. We could not believe that we were starting on our epic 4,500 mile flight across the Arctic and the Atlantic Ocean to Norwich. David Hughes

Leading 2nd Air Division veterans who arranged the great send-off at Meacham Field. l. to r. Geoff Gregory, 467th Bomb Group, Jordan Uttal, Headquarters.

and Ray Krottinger flew the first leg with Al Stricklin looking after the navigation and Sam Mangrum as flight engineer. The rest of us were back aft in the wartime canvas seats on each side of the waist gun positions in the rear of the fuselage.

Soon we were airborne into the low cloud with the typical Liberator gear retraction sequence and then we broke out into the blue sky and joined the airways at 9,000ft as we headed north over the states of Texas, Oklahoma, Kansas, Iowa and Minnesota. As we enjoyed our in-flight snacks and Coca-Cola, I realised what a great crew I was flying with. Four hours later we started our descent into the massive Minneapolis/St Paul International Airport mixed in with all the airline traffic. Fly-pasts were not allowed so we settled into the approach with gear and flaps down. Suddenly, to our surprise, the Tower asked us if we could do a fly-past, so it was gear and flaps up and we swept over the Terminal where we were just amazed to see the huge crowds waiting for us. Back to the final approach and David Hughes made a really smooth landing, followed by taxi instructions to the main NorthWest hangar. We made a great sight and sound as we passed the Main Terminal.

Three happy CAF Colonels ready for departure.
l. to r. Henry Brand, Flight Engineer, Roy Krottinger, Pilot, Sam Mangrum , Flight Engineer.

Arrival at Minneapolis/St Paul

At the NorthWest apron we saw crowds of people waiting for us and we parked beside a Boeing 747 with our flags proudly flying from the cockpit. As Sam Mangrum left the aircraft to place the Pogo stick under the tail (to prevent the B-24 from dropping back) he was presented with a huge bouquet of flowers, something we did not let him forget for the rest of the trip. Then we were all out into the sunshine to be greeted by the Chairman of NorthWest Airlines and Jane from their PR office. With them was Lt Al Dexter, my wartime Liberator pilot, with his wife Pat and all his family, so the links with history began again. NorthWest had made a huge welcome cake which we all enjoyed with cool drinks – what wonderful sponsors they were! The Chairman asked me what we were eating on the next day on our long haul into the Arctic. I showed him our small lunch boxes and he took one look and said he could do better than that; he would send a catering truck out to us early the next morning before our departure.

Then I was off with Jane from NorthWest to their Operations building for my first live broadcast to BBC Radio Norfolk with the good news that we were on our way home. Crowds of NorthWest employees wanted to see inside 'Diamond Lil' and talk to us, but eventually a crew bus arrived to take us to our superb rooms in the Airport Hilton Hotel. In the evening it got even better as they had arranged dinner in a private room, where we listened in awe to Al Dexter talking about his wartime flying experiences and how he met me as a schoolboy and lifted me over the fence to meet his crew and see his B-24 Liberator bomber. (See *David and the Mighty Eighth* by Marjorie Hodgson Parker.)

We are on our Way

The next morning all the crew saw the sun rise over the Missisippi before going down for a very early breakfast – it looked a great day for flying. However, at the crew breakfast, David Hughes, our Commander, dropped a bombshell. After much thought and studying the flight plan he had decided that our two girl Colonels would not fly the next three legs, but instead would fly from Minneapolis/St Paul to Prestwick and re-join the crew there. This brought howls of protest from our two girls, but David was adamant and in the end they saw the wisdom of his argument, but we would miss them. At 0700hrs, having visited NorthWest Operations to check the weather, notams and file our flight plan, we were back on the apron and walking out to 'Diamond Lil', who was still surrounded by dozens of NorthWest employees waiting to wish us good luck. As promised, a catering truck arrived and delivered some fantastic food hampers plus flasks of hot and cold drinks – what a sponsor we had. Lt Al Dexter was also there to wish us 'bon voyage'. He wished he was coming with us, but would meet us at Prestwick. We said a sad farewell to Starr and Kathy, signed the crew manifest, pulled the props through, completed a very thorough pre-flight check and then, with Henry Brand standing fireguard, we started the engines to begin our nine and a half hour flight to Iqaluit in Canada. The Tower gave us priority over all other traffic and airline passengers must have been surprised to see a wartime B-24 Liberator bomber taxiing past them on that super morning.

At 0830hrs we made our first max weight take-off at 58,000 lbs with our full fuel load of 3,000 gallons, but David Hughes made it all look so easy despite using up a lot of the runway. We soon settled into our cruise routine at 7,000ft. As we approached Lake Superior I was flying in the right hand seat when the Squadron played its routine trick on all new pilots. Once the off-duty Flight Engineers realised that I had settled in, they suddenly ran aft. Now the B-24 is very sensitive to fore and aft trim and to my horror the nose suddenly reared up. I looked to David Hughes in the left seat but he was staring out of his side window; no answer on the intercom, so I pushed hard down and re-trimmed, wondering what the heck had happened. As soon as the two jokers in the tail saw that I had re-trimmed they ran back to the bomb bay. This meant that the nose dropped; again no help from David, so I pulled hard back and re-trimmed, fearing that I had disgraced myself. When things seemed back to normal, Henry Brand appeared in the cockpit and said 'OK David, you have passed.' I won't repeat my reply.

We were flying in one-hour stints before going on to navigation or retiring to the rest area in the rear fuselage. I had brought out from the UK one of the original 2nd Air Division USAAF B-24 Liberator pilot's handbooks and this was in high demand. We watched with interest the BBC film crew interviewing Simon Bates then, deciding it was time for lunch, we opened the NorthWest lunch boxes to find a truly amazing variety of food that would last us for another two days – they had been so kind. Then, as we crossed into Canada, Al Stricklin announced that 'Diamond Lil' had left the United States en route for England. This brought a cheer from the crew and we stuck up the charts in our rest area aft so that everyone could follow our progress over the wild tundra in this exciting and barren part of Canada. We had not seen another aircraft for ages. At 1400hrs we had our first sight of the Arctic ice which was beautiful. The outside air temperature was now down to minus 15 degrees and we picked up some airframe icing in cloud. We had also discovered a problem up front as we had a vicious cold draught coming in through the nose which we could not cure, so we flew with a canvas sheet over our knees, but one hour was enough.

The beauty of the Arctic Circle on a perfect afternoon as we started the descent to Frobisher Bay.

What a wild part of the world this is, but the ice, the glaciers and the clouds made a lovely sight in the late afternoon sun as we cruised steadily on at 9,000ft, enjoying our NorthWest snacks. No sign of any polar bears, however.

Chapter 5

INTO THE ARCTIC

At 1630hrs, having enjoyed our NorthWest coffee and cookies, we started our descent into the lonely little airport in Frobisher Bay. I really had enjoyed flying 'Diamond Lil' and the scenery took your breath away as we flew up the frozen inlet leading to Iqaluit, lowering the gear and flaps as we turned on to final approach for the single 9,000ft runway. As always David Hughes made a 'greaser' of a landing looking at the small hutted town with a very modern Control Tower painted bright yellow. Parked at the refuelling point (no fuel trucks here) the

Colonel Ray Krottinger on the wing during the refuelling at Iqaluit. Note the yellow Control Tower.

view from the cockpit was stunning in the late afternoon sun, although for Sam Mangrum out on the wing it was a long, cold process. The charming Canadian Customs girl completed the formalities and then asked to have her picture taken against our famous aeroplane. Each of the crew received a highly-prized Arctic Circle Certificate and then we all had a chance to stand back, take photographs and admire our great Liberator, resting at last after over nine hours of flying. Refuelling complete, we had to taxi 'Diamond Lil' down to her overnight parking area where she would have to endure a very cold night as there was no spare hangar space at Iqaluit. We also saw a disappointing side of Simon Bates and the BBC crew as they offered no help but just vanished to their hotel.

'Diamond Lil' parked beside the snow at Iqaluit, engines shut down.

Waiting outside the Control Tower for our transport to the airport hotel, I came in for a lot of leg-pulling about my flying, but Ray Krottinger confirmed his faith in my ability so I could relax a little. The Airport Discovery Lodge was a very warm, but expensive, single storey building. The rooms were comfortable and we enjoyed a great crew dinner, happy that we had reached Iqaluit safely. We turned in early, ready for the next exciting leg across the Arctic – for me it still seemed unreal. I never thought that I would ever fly in the Arctic Circle, let alone in a B-24 Liberator. What a life!

The crew of 'Diamond Lil' enjoying supper at the Discovery Lodge, Iqaluit.

'You guys are on your own now'

The next day, Wednesday June 3rd, we enjoyed a hearty Canadian breakfast, followed by a thorough crew briefing, including a warning to wear all our warm clothing. David and Ray checked the Met, notams and filed our flight plan and then 'Diamond Lil' was pulled into the specially heated hangar for the vital two-hour warm-up after a night outside in very low temperatures. We were number two in the hangar behind a Boeing 737 and it cost the CAF a small fortune, but it had to be done. At 0900hrs the hangar door opened and 'Diamond Lil' was pulled out into the sunshine. We completed a careful pre-flight, pulled the props through and settled back in that comfortable cockpit once more at the beginning of the most challenging part of our journey, the nine-hour flight across Greenland. Then we hit a snag as there was no sign of Simon Bates and the BBC film crew – not what we wanted. David Hughes decided to start to taxi. Suddenly they appeared and, opening the aft door to let them in, we were horrified to see that Simon Bates was only wearing a thin T-shirt and jeans.

We made our way out to the runway and prepared for another max weight take-off. Climbing out, you realised just how wild and barren this part of the world is; the Canadian Radar Controller summed it up when he said goodbye and added, 'You guys are on your own now'.

The Arctic icecap was truly beautiful as we climbed slowly up to 9,000ft and we enjoyed the beauty of the mountains and glaciers, then later the ice-floes and icebergs as we entered the Davis Strait. The outside air temperature was now down to minus 21 degrees, but the heaters were working well as the inside temperature was up to minus 5 degrees. We were all glad of our warm clothing, all that is except Simon Bates, who was interviewed shivering with cold and telling his TV audience that it was 'freezing cold up here in the Arctic', while the rest of us sat just out of camera shot, nice and warm in our parkas. We realised then why he had ignored the briefing and was not wearing proper clothing, just to make the story more interesting.

Soon we approached the mountains and glaciers on the west coast of Greenland, looking much more impressive than when I last saw them from the 747 at 37,000ft, but certainly not the place for a forced

Approaching the awesome mountains of Greenland – not the place for a forced landing.

landing. We kept a sharp lookout for polar bears, but had no luck. Then we passed within a few miles of where they were digging a B-17 Flying Fortress and some P-38 Lightning fighters out of the ice where they had crashed during a wartime delivery flight. Here we appreciated the kindness of one of our sponsors who had fitted a GPS in the cockpit, as the compass began some wild swings as we neared the North Pole, though our confidence was shaken when it displayed the message 'down for maintenance' for about twenty minutes. None of us had ever seen the Arctic Icecap at low level before and it was quite featureless, so we were glad when the GPS came back on line, but the scenery was breathtaking.

Engine Failure

Just as I was finishing my spell on the flight deck we noticed a rise in the temperature of the No.1 engine and we opened the gills. This seemed to help and I returned aft to have a rest and a cup of NorthWest coffee when suddenly I noticed that oil seemed to be leaking from No.1 engine. I pointed this out to Sam Mangrum, also off watch, and he vanished in a flash to the cockpit with me hard on his heels. When we told David Hughes what we had seen, and of the increase in cylinder head temperatures, he wisely decided to shut down the engine and feather the propeller. So now we had to decide what we had to do. Should we turn around and fight the headwinds all the way back to Iqaluit, with some doubt as to what servicing facilities might be available, or should we carry on to Keflavik and the US Navy? We decided to carry on and I returned aft where Simon Bates was reading his book. I asked him if he had looked out of my side of the aircraft recently. He said, 'No, why?' and I told him that we had just stopped the No.1 engine and feathered the propeller. His face dropped and he was 'white knuckled' for the next four and a half hours! Al Stricklin then came aft to brief the BBC crew and our two passengers on what had happened and the decision they had taken to carry on to Iceland on three engines and slowly climb up to 11,000ft. He advised them to 'Stay warm and cool.'

The No.1 engine stopped and propeller feathered over the Arctic Icecap. *Courtesy RAF Kinloss*

Later, when I was back in the right seat, we had another problem. Cloud formed, totally unforecast, and we could not climb above it with ice forming on the feathered propeller. Ray Krottinger tried everything he knew to get the old lady to climb, but she would have none of it. Then we suddenly burst out into the blue sky once more and the ice vanished, but that was some experience for this new B-24 pilot. Still the scenery was stunning as we passed the Sea Bass reporting point and relayed our position via the Boeing 747s high above us. At one point I was happily telling a 747 that we were a wartime B-24 Liberator returning to England when Ray Krottinger told me that I was talking to German Lufthansa aircraft! Then it was time to go back aft and enjoy a late NorthWest lunch. To port you could still see the Arctic Icecap as we approached the snow-covered mountains on the east coast of Greenland (with a very quiet BBC crew and presenter). Now we could see the glaciers and ice-floes as we approached the Denmark Strait and we were all overwhelmed by the magnificence of the Arctic sunset; the sun glinting on the ice was truly wonderful.

The glorious Arctic sunset as we approached the Denmark Strait on three engines.

At last we cleared the mountains and descended back to 9,000ft and it was then that we began to realise what it must have been like to limp home in the '40s on three engines. At least we did not have any hostile fighters or flak to contend with. Now, with great relief we were talking to the tower at Keflavik; they cleared us down to 5,000ft and to our surprise there was not a single ship in the Denmark Strait. The cameras were working overtime as we approached the tops of the cumulus clouds and took one last look at that unbelievable sunset, a memory that is still with us today. Who else has seen a B-24 tail-fin against that backdrop? We could hardly believe that we had crossed the Arctic Icecap on three engines. We had detailed discussions on the possible cause of the failure of our No.1 engine and hoped that it was something simple like an oil leak; we were worried about a possible delay to our planned arrival time in the UK and Norwich.

David Hughes landing 'Diamond Lil' on three engines in the rain at Keflavik.

Courtesy RAF Kinloss

Arrival in Iceland

Once below the broken cloud, we could see the welcome sight of the coast of Iceland and, while we relaxed, David and Ray prepared to cope with a crosswind landing in the rain on three engines. At 2230hrs local David made a really smooth landing and as we taxied into the US Navy ramp we were followed by all the crash vehicles with their flashing lights, quite a sight. We came to a stop with the 120 Squadron Nimrod from Kinloss in the background and we realised that the worst of the journey was over. Wing Commander Mitch Lees, the 120 Squadron Boss, was there to meet us, as was Flt Lt Steve Rennison, who had been a great liaison officer – it was really good to meet them. The crew then had to face a battery of television cameras and radio reporters. We gathered that it was not often that a B-24 Liberator landed at Keflavik on three engines. We were also glad that our two girl Scanners had not had to endure that experience. David's decision had certainly proved to be a wise one. The US Navy was great and soon 'Diamond Lil' was towed into a warm US Navy Orion Squadron hangar and it was all hands on deck to discover the problem with our No.1 engine. As always Simon Bates and the BBC crew vanished, but about 30 minutes later an American girl sailor ran across the hangar to tell us to come quickly as the CNN news channel had just had a news flash that Simon Bates would be talking about 'the day he almost died'. We crammed into their small crew-room and to our amazement there was Simon Bates saying that 'we had an engine explode over Greenland and we plummeted down towards the mountains.' David Hughes was furious as this was playing with his career, and the truth was that we had stopped the engine to save it, feathered the propeller as normal and climbed up to 11,000ft. We were also concerned that Simon Bates had got on to CNN as we had been assured that he was purely BBC and not freelance. Any work outside the BBC would invalidate our insurance and that of the Nimrod.

So ended two remarkable days of flying that we would never forget, the first time for all of us at low level in the Arctic Circle. The send-off from Minneapolis/St Paul had been a memorable occasion and the food from NorthWest Airlines had enabled us to eat and drink to a very high standard throughout the journey. Then we had experienced the amazing barren and wild tundra of Northern Canada, the ice-floes and the huge drop in outside air temperature causing airframe icing in cloud. The frozen inlet leading up to Iqaluit on Frobisher Bay with its 9,000ft runway was also quite something. We can never forget the kindness of everyone at Iqaluit or the huge cost of having 'Diamond Lil' warmed up the next morning after her night out in the cold. Later on we were convinced that most of our engine troubles had been caused by that night in low temperatures.

The flight out the next day started on a high note when the Canadian Controller said goodbye as we left his zone and added, 'You guys are on your own now'. How right he was. Our first sight of the awesome mountains on the west coast of Greenland, followed by the amazing featureless icecap, made us realise what we had taken on. No wonder that aircraft got lost during the war – we were glad of our GPS.

A very happy and relieved crew after landing at Keflavik. With them are the crew from No.120 Squadron Nimrod and the BBC camera team. Note the oil streaks on the port fin from the failed No. 1 engine.

Courtesy of RAF Kinloss

The engine failure had showed just how lucky I was to be flying with such an experienced crew and later events would prove how correct our decision had been to carry onto Keflavik. I learnt so much from watching Ray Krottinger's efforts to get 'Diamond Lil' to climb out of the cloud on three engines. Losing the No.1 engine made all on board think about the dangers we were now facing. If we lost a second engine, we would have to throw out all the spare kit, and if another one went it would have meant a forced landing on the icecap – another unknown situation. If we survived the landing intact, how long would it be before we were rescued? Did we have enough food and drink to last, and was our warm clothing going to be good enough? And what about polar bears? Luckily our three engines performed superbly and we settled down to make the best of the task of limping home to Keflavik, but it certainly left us with memories of a lifetime. Finally we had that Arctic sunset, which had us all spellbound, the perfect landing by David Hughes, and that amazing greeting at Keflavik from the RAF Nimrod crew and the US Navy – two days that will never be forgotten.

Chapter 6

WITH THE US NAVY AT KEFLAVIK

Now it was back to work to find the problem. We undid the cowlings on our No.1 engine, hoping to see signs of an oil leak which we knew we could cure easily. Sadly, no trace of a leak, so the oil screens were opened and there, as we feared, were particles of metal, meaning we had a major problem. The US Navy engineers from Orion Squadron, who had offered to help us throughout the night, were superb, and indeed said how great it was to work on a 'round' engine again. They sent the metal particles away for analysis and within 30 minutes came back with the bad news that we had traces of copper and silver, which meant that a main bearing had gone. This left us with no option but to remove first the propeller and then the engine. Being just a pilot, all I could do was to hand up the tools as required and collect the old oil. But I certainly learnt a lot about engine-changing. A very attractive US Navy girl sailor appeared and asked if we would be working through the night. When we said yes, she told us that three of them would prepare meals for us in their crew-room as the Transit Mess was miles away from the hangar. They were great, as were the engineers with their lifting equipment. We had certainly made the right decision to carry on to Keflavik as the US Navy shared our determination to get 'Diamond Lil' on her way to the UK as soon as possible.

The comfortable US Navy Transit Aircrew quarters at Keflavik, our home for three days.

By 0300hrs the engine and propeller were on the hangar floor and a very tired crew retired to the Transit Mess. I was lucky enough to share a room with David Kjell, our Senior Flight Engineer. Henry Brand had told me to get him to show me his Engineer's licence and when I asked David he just smiled and I was amazed to see that he was cleared by the FAA to work on almost every type of aircraft in the western world. He was in great demand, as we would shortly find out.

At breakfast in the very comfortable Mess it was agreed that we would have to get our spare engine flown out from Mildenhall. The RAF Liaison Officer on the Base kindly offered us the use of his office and any other facility we needed. The US Navy asked if we were happy with a charge of a dollar a meal and a dollar a night in the Mess which we all thought was very reasonable – what friends they were.

Sorting out the problems

In the Liaison Officer's office Al Stricklin made the call to Fort Worth to give the Squadron and the CAF the news of our problems and to check that the spare engine was at Mildenhall as planned. Here we had a huge shock. The Squadron told us that a very officious USAF Lt Colonel had refused to fly the engine to the UK as we 'did not have the right signatures'. Al phoned him but he was still adamant and was obviously not interested in the CAF or the 50th anniversary project. We could not contact the US General in charge of SAC so Al suggested that I might try our Air Vice Marshal Sir John (Kip) Kemball. I was straight on the telephone and luckily Sir John was in his office. I explained our problems and asked if he knew the US General. We were in luck as Kip did know him and had served with him on an exchange tour, so would phone him and call us later. Within an hour Kip was back with the good news that he had spoken to the General and he had authorised the flight of our spare engine. We phoned the USAAF Lt Colonel who was responsible for the shipping, thinking he would be pleased, but he was still determined to be difficult, saying that the authorisation was from *Charleston* to Keflavik and that we had just 24 hours to get the engine shipped from Fort Worth in Texas to Charleston in South Carolina. Al Stricklin was left with the task of finding a trucker who was prepared to drive non-stop for 24 hours. Most companies he phoned turned us down, but eventually he found a small 'father and son' operation who agreed to try, but could not guarantee to meet the deadline. We phoned our dear USAF Lt Colonel back with the news, but all he did was confirm that he would not hold the flight – what a nightmare this had become.

While we were doing all this, the rest of the crew were stripping and cleaning all the accessories, carburettors and oil coolers off the old engine ready to be fitted to the new one. We also cleaned 'Diamond Lil' from nose to tail. Also on that day we had a chance to express our anger to the BBC Producer about the Simon Bates interview on CNN and some of the crew almost came to blows with him. Sadly, one of our sponsor passengers had to return to the UK, so Wing Commander Mitch Lees, the 120 Squadron Commander, offered him a seat on Nimrod, which also had to return to UK. He promised to return as soon as we were ready to depart. Then Simon Bates demanded that 120 Squadron should fly him home. Initially he was told that the Nimrod was full, but when he discovered that our sponsor was flying he insisted that he should have his place. The Squadron crew were not happy with this, but Simon Bates created such a fuss that in the end they relented and our sponsor had to make his own way home on scheduled airlines. Bates promised he would be back, but he never turned up, which, as Sam Mangrum said, 'was a pity as half way over the Atlantic he would have plummeted down after being pushed out'. Worse was to come later when we discovered that the video tape programme on our flight, which was part of the deal, did not materialise.

That evening I was saved by David Kjell. He had found out that the crew intended to catch me out in the bar before dinner. Their tradition was that each member of the crew should undo his flight jacket to display his Confederate Air Force belt buckle; anyone who couldn't do this bought the drinks. They knew only too well that I didn't have a buckle. David said he had a spare silver-plated buckle an insisted that I wear it. (Later on he gave it to me as a gift which I still treasure.) So down in the bar, when all the crew opened their jackets with a yell, they were stunned to see that I too was wearing a buckle! Later that evening, the US Navy Orion Squadron insisted that we visit their Mess and we enjoyed a hilarious evening, a welcome relief after the horrendous task of trying to get our spare engine on its way.

David Kjell with the author.

The next morning the crew decided to tour the island while Al Stricklin and I spent the day in the RAF Liaison Officer's office checking on the progress of the engine and making all the necessary changes to our programme. First we had to give Prestwick the sad news that we would not make their air show or the link-up with the Red Arrows and the Spitfire. Next we had to give my Jean a huge task as she had to make all the other changes in the UK, including Prestwick, the Media, the hotels and also notify all the sponsors who were due to fly on the Base Flights of the revised times. She had also to arrange for Al and Pat Dexter and the two girl Colonels to be flown from Prestwick to Norwich and then look after them. We gave her a real nightmare, but luckily Squadron Leader Berry Savory stepped in to help. Finally I did my live broadcast to BBC Radio Norfolk, but Jean said that I sounded tired!

Later that day we checked with the USAF at Charleston to see if our engine had arrived, but they had seen no sign of it. The flight they were using was the scheduled one to Iceland, Mildenhall and Germany and could not easily be delayed. Luckily the aircraft Commander turned out to be a true friend and agreed to snag the aircraft for at least an hour, but we could not contact our trucker. Back to Charleston where we got the sad news that our engine had not arrived so they had to let the flight depart. Then came the good news. The USAF officer in charge at Charleston went on to say, 'I don't know just who you guys know, but your engine is being flown out specially as soon as it arrives.' What a joy it was to have an RAF Air Vice Marshall and a USAF General on the team – we can never thank them enough.

Our New Engine Arrives

On Monday June 8th a huge USAF Starlifter taxied up to our hangar and, when the nose opened up, there inside was one small pallet with our engine and tyres – what a relief! So it was all hands to unpacking the engine to get it ready for fitting; once again the US Navy Orion Squadron engineers were superb. There was one small snag: we needed to re-torque the propeller, but they did not have the required

'Diamond Lil' in the US Navy Orion hangar on the first night – starting the engine change.

Unpacking the new engine. l. to r. Sam Mangrum, Ray Krottinger and Al Stricklin.

The new engine on the wing in the Orion hangar.

Pratt & Whitney spanner. After some quick phone-calls, however, we located a small Icelandic airline that operated a C-47 Dakota using Pratt & Whitneys and they willingly agreed to deliver the tool to us. Later that night all the work was complete and we retired to our rooms in the Transit Mess utterly exhausted. We then had another blow. Our Chief Engineer, David Kjell, had a call from the FAA in the States to say that he was urgently needed in Switzerland to deal with a Learjet problem at Zurich Airport and had to leave us.

Tuesday June 9th and the lifting of the new engine and propeller began, aided by a brilliant Master Sergeant in the US Navy who could really drive a crane. This was where I realised the huge advantage of working with a CAF crew who were all qualified engineers and after 32 hours of very hard work we were all smiling again. They had certainly taught me a great deal. Thank goodness we had not decided to change the engine at Iqaluit. We noticed that overnight our Liberator had been zapped by a Dutch Orion crew as we had a neat Dutch flag added to the row beneath the cockpit window. Finally we retired to the Orion Squadron Mess for a celebration supper, the whole company delighted to see that we had all four engines on the wings once more, a real team effort to get us on our way again.

Nimrod and Liberator crews at the US Navy flight briefing for the Atlantic crossing

At 2330hrs in the Arctic twilight, 'Diamond Lil' was pushed out of the Orion hangar ready to start the new engine. Thanks to our wonderful engineers, *she started the first time* and soon settled down to the cheers of the many onlookers. All the checks were now complete, cowlings replaced and secured and the BP tanker arrived to refuel us before we towed 'Diamond Lil' back into the hangar. We tidied up our mess, cleaned the hangar floor and said a very sincere 'thank you' to all the engineers who had worked with us and to the girl sailors who had fed us so well. At 0200hrs we retired to bed, with a warning from David Hughes to be down for breakfast at 0700hrs.

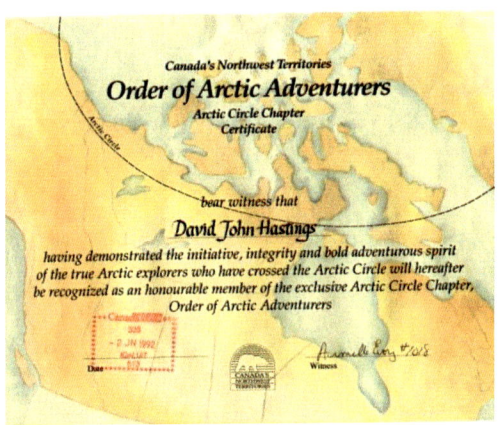

The highly prized Arctic Circle Certificate presented to each member of the 'Diamond Lil' crew at Iqaluit.

Wednesday June 10th, after a good breakfast we packed up all our kit and vacated our rooms in the Transit Mess and were overjoyed to see the 120 Squadron Nimrod, with Wing Commander Mitch Lees, back on the apron outside our hangar. We were so pleased to see them all once again. I made a last visit to the RAF Liaison office to speak to BBC Radio Norfolk to let the county know that we were on our way and hoped to be there by teatime; without our Prestwick visit we would be flying direct to Norwich after our forty-five minute customs stop at RAF Kinloss. The sun was shining for the first time since we had arrived in Iceland and the next thing for both the Liberator and Nimrod crews was the US Navy Met briefing and flight planning ready for the longest overwater leg in our journey, estimated at just under five hours. At the briefing Mitch Lees said that, in view of all the hard work done by Flt Lt Steve Rennison, he would like him to fly with us, the only current Nimrod pilot to fly a B-24 Liberator – he was overjoyed. To have Steve on board with us was another dream come true for the crew of 'Diamond Lil'. Then it was back to the Orion hangar to get our famous Liberator out into the sunshine. It seemed as though the entire base had turned out to see us on our way.

We can never express our thanks enough to everyone on the Base at Keflavik for their determination to get us on our way again to the UK and the wonderful way they looked after us. We were just so lucky.

**Taking off from Keflavik on a fine morning.
The start of the Atlantic crossing.**

Chapter 7

THE ATLANTIC CROSSING

By 0935hrs we were back with 'Diamond Lil', had loaded all the kit and had a very thorough pre-flight, including the now regular routine of pulling the props through. Then we started the engines and taxied away to the active runway receiving a fond farewell from the huge crowd of US Navy and RAF personnel who had looked after us so well. At the holding point it was good to see our escorting Nimrod on the other side and it was a great comfort to know that they would be with us all the way across the Atlantic to Kinloss, although at the briefing they had kindly said that if we had a major problem they would 'film us all the way down'. As we knew from the B-24 Manual our chance of surviving a ditching in the Atlantic was pretty low, but on such a morning we did not want to know about that. All we knew was that we were on our way to Norwich at last.

It was a really super morning for flying and at 1035hrs we lifted off from Keflavik, past the US Navy Orion hangar with the new No.1 engine running well as we climbed up to our altitude of 9,000ft. Unbelievably we were on the last leg of our historic flight. Then, as we crossed the coast of Iceland, the Nimrod escort closed up to starboard.

The wonderful sight of the 120 Squadron Nimrod escort closing up to starboard.

What a wonderful team 120 Squadron had been, and how strange that fifty years ago our Liberator should have been flying with the Squadron. We all watched with pride as Steve Rennison took over the left seat; he really enjoyed flying our B-24 and deserved it. Then it was my turn to fly the old lady and what a sight the Pratt & Whitneys made from the left hand seat. Ray Krottinger enjoyed watching my efforts to hold

**The author flying 'Diamond Lil' over the Atlantic.
Note the 467th shoulder patch.**

height and heading – what a true friend he had been to me. Now we were above solid cloud cover and the second Nimrod, carrying all the world press and TV, joined up to port. Ray warned me not to watch him, but just to maintain height and heading. We changed crews and I returned aft to grab my camera just as the TV cameramen in the second Nimrod asked them to get closer. As the photographs proved, he did get close, but it was a superb piece of formation flying and we were lucky to have such an escort over the Atlantic – the moist air produced some stunning contrails from his wingtips. Steve Rennison was interviewed by the BBC and asked about the difference between flying a Nimrod and a B-24.

With the photo session over both Nimrods formated on us to starboard as we enjoyed the last of the NorthWest Pepsi and cookies. By 1400hrs the coast of Scotland was in sight as we passed over Stornaway. We all breathed a sigh of relief that the Atlantic crossing was over, but what a memory! The 'Press' Nimrod then left us and the Squadron Boss formated on us to starboard as we started our descent towards RAF Kinloss through the rapidly building cumulus clouds. With the

Flight Lt Steve Rennison of No.120 Squadron being interviewed on board by the BBC.

airfield now in sight our formation closed up ready for a low fly-past to thank the Squadron and the Station, followed by a run-in and break for landing on runway 08, casting a unique shadow on the sands. This was the first time a B-24 Liberator had been seen at Kinloss for over forty years.

The second Nimrod, with the world press on board, did get quite close to port.

Arrival at RAF Kinloss

As always David Hughes made a 'greaser' of a landing and we taxied slowly past the Tower to a tremendous greeting from the Station. As we stepped out into the sunshine we were greeted by a piper and then officially received our delivery certificate, noting that we were just fifty-one years, one week and one day late. We met up with a Jaguar pilot from RAF Coltishall and also our Customs Officer. Here we met a snag as his boss decided that he too wanted to see 'Diamond Lil', so our clearance had to be 'by the book'. This meant that all stores and spare parts in the nose and bomb bay had to be inspected, so instead of forty-five minutes it took one and a half hours, necessitating another frantic phone call to Jean to advise her of the delay in our arrival at Norwich. Now it was time to thank the Squadron, but some of the crews wanted to join us on the flight to Norwich so we welcomed them on board. Airborne once more we turned east. RAF Lossiemouth asked if we could give them a fly-past, so we obliged with a very low pass down their main runway. Then we climbed back up to 9,000ft on a perfect afternoon with Military Radar clearance all the way to Norwich.

Greeted by a piper at RAF Kinloss. l. to r. David Hughes, Ray Krottinger, the Piper, Henry Brand, Sam Mangrum, Al Stricklin.

We crossed the Firth of Forth, then the Tyne, navigation being very easy for me as we had perfect weather and we had the skies to ourselves. For the Americans this was strange scenery, but we all began to relax in the beautiful early evening sun, knowing that we were nearly home after 4,500 miles of some of the most challenging flying of my life with a truly wonderful crew. As we crossed over into Lincolnshire we saw the final gift from Air Marshall Sir John Kemball. Three Jaguars from No.41 Squadron at Coltishall swept up out of the clouds to formate on each wing and the tail – just unbelievable! The painting in the Mess at Coltishall, 'Welcome Home Yank', had really come alive. I don't think there was a dry eye on board. It was all so emotional and was indeed 'Welcome Home Yank', a unique formation that would never be repeated. Air Traffic gave us a new call sign, 'Rebel Formation', very apt for a CAF aircraft. Suddenly, we heard a RAF Tornado asking for permission to join us and we welcomed him as it gave us yet another striking formation. He really tucked in tight with our Jaguars. One of the Jaguars, a two-seat version, which was flown by a great friend of mine (and well known aviation artist) Squadron Leader Mike Rondot,

What a wonderful sight the Jaguars of No. 41 Squadron made as they tucked in tight. The historic formation as 'Diamond Lil' arrived back home at Norwich International Airport. It was indeed 'Welcome Home Yank.'

Courtesy Archant, Eastern Daily Press

had a cameraman on board who produced some spectacular photographs to remind us all of this unique and never-to-be-repeated occasion. One of these photographs has pride of place in our home at Salhouse, just another reminder of the friendship and kindness of RAF Coltishall. Who would ever have thought that in 1992 a B-24 Liberator would be back in the skies over Norfolk?

Back in Norfolk at Last

At 1900hrs local, Air Traffic cleared our formation down to 1,500ft so that Norfolk could enjoy once more the sight and sound of a Liberator. We flew over a group of 2nd Air Division veterans who were visiting King's Lynn and were delighted to see us. We now aimed to route over as many of the old 2nd Air Division USAAF bases as we could and an ITV camera plane joined us. He requested us to 'slow up', but before we could reply he was answered by a call from a Jaguar pilot saying, 'Don't you dare!' First we flew over North Pickenham, the home of the 492nd Bomb Group, then Wendling, the home of the 392nd Bomb Group and finally Attlebridge, home of the 466th Bomb Group, now the site of the turkey sheds of one of our main sponsors, Bernard Matthews.

Chapter 8

THE ARRIVAL AT NORWICH

As we started our descent towards runway 09 at Norwich, wartime home of the 458th Bomb Group, with the evening sun glinting on our wings the formation closed up. We were briefed for a fly-past followed by a right turn to fly around the City, before lining up for a further fly-past at RAF Coltishall on runway 04. Huge crowds were lining our airport, which brought the comment from David Hughes, 'You didn't tell me we were landing on a car park'. Then sadly it all fell apart as the girl in the Tower at Norwich was so overcome with emotion that she cleared us to turn left instead of right. This ruined our fly-past over the City, but Ray Krottinger rightly said, 'David, don't get her to change our direction with a formation this tight.' So we headed out towards the coast before turning west to line up with runway 22 at RAF Coltishall. Ray asked how low we could go. I told him it was a military airfield so it was up to him. He started on down only to receive a call from one of the Jaguars asking him how much lower he was going. When Ray asked why, the Jaguar pilot informed him that he was under our tail! Still it was an impressive fly-past to thank the station for their wonderful support. Now we lowered the gear for the last time as we turned over Attlebridge for our landing on runway 09 at Norwich International Airport. We were staggered to see the huge crowds as we crossed the threshold. Yet another smooth landing from David Hughes and as we backtracked down the runway we proudly placed our two flags, the Stars and Stripes and the Union Jack outside the cockpit. There to meet us was a wartime 'follow me' jeep to lead us into our dispersal on the disused runway and to the crowds waiting for us. We could not believe that we had achieved our dream in the fiftieth anniversary year.

Once on the chocks, we completed the checks and then shut down the engines before all the crew stepped out into the evening sun and, true to tradition, Sam Mangrum was presented with a huge bouquet of

**The huge crowds waiting to see over 'Diamond Lil'
after her arrival at Norwich.**

flowers – the word had obviously spread to Norwich. Al and Pat Dexter were there and Starr and Cathy and the CAF UK support crew, also my daughter and grandson with Christopher holding up a large sign saying 'Welcome home, Grandad'. Leslie Woolf, Chairman of Broadland District Council and Laurie Sear, Editor of the *Eastern Daily Press*, were also there. The words of welcome from Tom Eaton, Memorial Trust Chairman, touched us all. It seemed a long time since he had told me to find a B-24 and bring it to Great Britain. David Hughes replied on behalf of the crew and I thanked the Confederate Air Force before presenting the Heritage League scroll to the 1st Taverham Scout Group. Jean had worked so hard on all the arrangements – everything was perfect despite all the delays and last minute changes.

Now the crew had to pose for the photographers in front of 'Diamond Lil' and we had to endure a whole series of TV and Radio interviews before we could finally relax with a glass of champagne kindly provided by Air UK. What a joy it was to see Al and Pat Dexter and we sat together in the cockpit for the first time in over forty years while they gave a film interview. Then the hundreds of people who had been invited to the apron all wanted to be shown on board, collect our autographs and buy the souvenirs, so a very tired crew just kept going until it was dark. What touched us all was the number of youngsters, who knew nothing about the War, but kept coming up and saying that they just had to touch a B-24 Liberator.

On to the Norwich Sport Village to relax at last and enjoy a very welcome supper with a glass of beer with Tom Eaton's words ringing in our ears: 'So, fifty years on, in 1992, a Liberator has returned to Norfolk, thanks to the Confederate Air Force and a gallant crew, in a tribute to the men and women of the 2nd Air Division who first arrived in 1942 to fight for freedom. They came as friends, they stayed as friends, and they have remained friends, and we will always remember them with pride and affection.'

We slept well that night, our duty done.

The crew of 'Diamond Lil' photographed on their arrival
at Norwich with the author's grandson.
l. to r. Ray Krottinger, Sam Mangrum, Henry Brand, Al Stricklin,
David Hughes, kneeling Christopher Hart and David Hastings.

One very happy pilot in the cockpit of 'Diamond Lil'
after landing at Norwich.

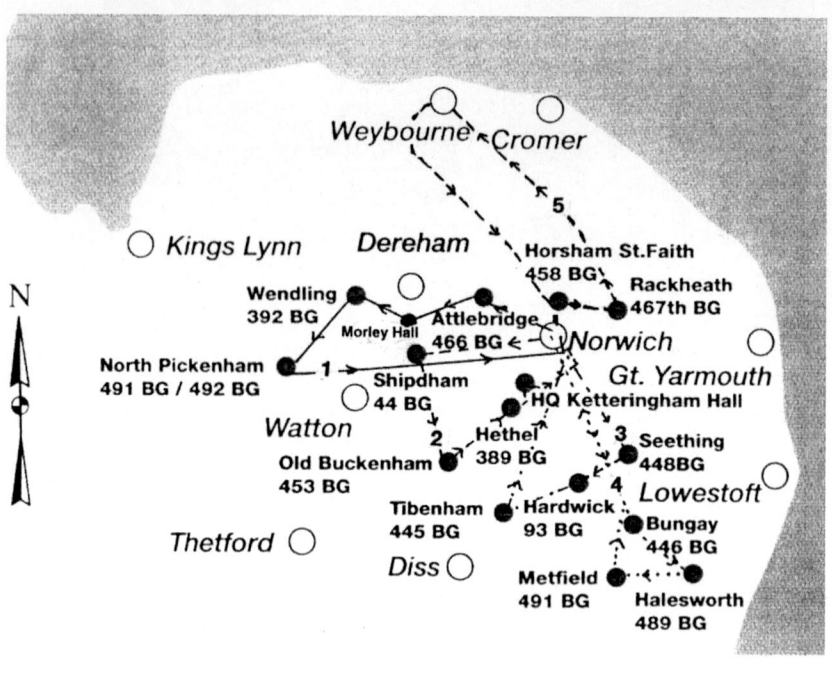

The routes flown on the five Base Tour flights from Norwich International Airport

_____ (1) Attlebridge, Morley Hall (Wymondham College), Wendling, North Pickenham

_ _ _ _ (2) Shipdham, Old Buckenham, Ketteringham Hall, Hethel

_ . _ . _ . (3) Seething, Hardwick, Tibenham

. . . . (4) Bungay, Halesworth, Metfield

_ _ _ _ (5) Horsham St.Faith, Rackheath, Muckleburgh, Langham

Average duration of each flight one hour, cruising height 3,000ft with low pass over the bases

Map of the Base Tour flights.

Chapter 9

THE BASE TRIBUTES AND THE TOUR

Once rested, we had to start the tribute flights over all the old 2nd Air Division bases, but first we wanted to thank the Confederate Air Force crew for all their kindness, so various special visits were planned. The Lord Mayor of Norwich welcomed them to the City and they visited the unique 2nd Air Division USAAF Memorial Library. Bernard Matthews personally greeted them at Great Witchingham Hall – what a great supporter he had been. They had an exciting morning driving the cars at the Lotus factory at Hethel, and had a Norfolk pub lunch at the Salhouse Bell before each having a turn at driving a steam locomotive on the Bure Valley Railway. On one evening the Memorial Trust gave them dinner at the Hotel Norwich when the crew presented a series of photographs to the Memorial Library and on another evening they had supper with the Traffords at Broad House, Wroxham. Finally, the Norfolk Vintage Pilots gave them a memorable dinner at the Muckleburgh Collection, thanks to Berry Savory, complete with the Sheringham Shantymen.

Back to the tribute flights. While I enjoyed the navigation, Jean had to cope with all the sponsors arriving at Norwich International Airport for their free flights. We planned to visit the bases in batches of three or four, which meant that the sponsors enjoyed a flight of well over an hour. All were made at low level under strict Air Traffic control, but we were joined on several occasions by military aircraft who wished to get a close look at us. The groups were as follows:

1. Attlebridge (466th), Morley Hospital – Wymondham College (351st), Wendling (392nd), North Pickenham (492nd)
2. Shipdham (44th), Old Buckenham (453rd), Ketteringham Hall (HQ), Hethel (389th)
3. Seething (448th), Hardwick (93rd), Tibenham (445th)
4. Bungay (446th), Halesworth (489th), Metfield (491st),
5. Horsham St Faith (458th), Rackheath (467th), Muckleburgh.

The crew at Great Witchingham Hall to thank one of our main sponsors, Bernard Matthews.

The 'Diamond Lil' crew visit the Bure Valley Railway.
l. to r. standing - David Kjell, Starr Stone, Ray Krottinger, Al Stricklin, Henry Brand, kneeling – Kathy Martin, David Hastings, Sam Mangrum.

In order to thank Squadron Leader Berry Savory, we promised to fly him over Muckleburgh. When this news got out, the Headmaster of nearby Langham School asked us to fly over his school. I agreed, but was a bit worried about finding it. However, we did and to our surprise we saw that the whole school had formed up on their playing field in the shape of a diamond and 'Lil' – what a touching moment that was and Berry was delighted. That morning we also had Al Dexter on board to achieve our personal dream of flying together in a B-24 – 'goosebump time' as Al called it. Later, when we carried Pat Everson over Seething, where she had devoted so much of her life to preserving the memory of the Americans, as we swept low over the field her face was a picture. Shipdham was another vivid memory as, after our first pass, the owner, my friend Nigel Wright, called up on the R/T to ask if we could make another low pass. Ray Krottinger checked with me how low we could go and I confirmed that, as it was an active airfield, we could legally do an approach and overshoot. I still have a photograph looking down on 'Diamond Lil' that was taken from the Tower. Hardwick was another great memory, as was Tibenham, and the most staggering thing was that at each base and village there were hundreds of people in the streets and the fields waving flags. The response was amazing and we were inundated with requests to repeat these five flights.

Despite the huge cost of the fuel, the Confederate B-29/B-24 Squadron, led by Colonel Ray Krottinger, willingly agreed to the repeat so long as I would navigate. Although I thought I knew my county like the back of my hand, some of the old bases were not easy to find, but luckily we did not get lost once. I dread to think of the comments of the crew if I had been 'uncertain of our position' in my own area. I have to admit one 'error of navigation' that made the crew smile; if we were landing to the west, I always extended the downwind leg so that we flew over our home at Salhouse! We did, however, have one interesting afternoon when a flight was cancelled owing to weather. The Tower advised us that it might improve by late afternoon. Jean meanwhile was looking after a group of very disappointed sponsors in the Airport Terminal. David Hughes did not want to let them down, so we told Jean to tell them that we were willing to fly circuits of Norwich Airport, but they would be in cloud most of the time – what did they think?

The 'Diamond Lil' crew on a visit to Lotus Cars at Hethel.

Al Stricklin presents the 'Diamond Lil' picture to Tom Eaton, Memorial Trust Chairman, at the Hotel Norwich dinner.

Staggeringly, Jean said that they all wanted to fly regardless of the weather. So the coach brought them out and we launched off, with David saying he would welcome some instrument time and ILS approaches. We were into cloud almost immediately after take-off, but they had brief glimpses of the City through gaps in the cloud on the downwind leg, and then they saw an ILS for real before overshooting and landing on the next approach. We thought they would leave very disappointed, but they loved it. Sadly we could not fly our grandson as he was too young, but our son Roger flew and our daughter Carol, then pregnant with Alisha, so she also flew.

The usual drill for all the Base Tribute flights was to start from our parking apron at Norwich, which meant that Jean had to bus the first group out to us. They then had a full safety briefing before being strapped in aft ready for take-off. Once we had reached our cruising altitude, normally 3,000ft, we would invite them, two at a time, to visit the cockpit, which for many was the high-spot, although they said that just to be flying in a B-24 Liberator was the most important thing as it brought back memories of the 40s and their American friends. After landing we would stop at the Airport Terminal to collect the next group. For the crew it was a truly rewarding experience and we loved every minute.

Memories of the UK Tour

Sadly I did not see too much of the UK Tour as I had to get back to my business, but we saw 'Diamond Lil' off from Norwich on her way to Dunkeswell with one very lucky sponsor on board. At the RAF Swanton Morley Air Show I was the commentator on the ground and Lt Al Dexter was on board with his wife, Pat. Then at Biggin Hill Air Show the crew had another disaster – the No.3 engine failed. Frantic efforts to obtain another engine in the UK were unsuccessful so the Squadron had to strip an engine from a Catalina in the USA and ship it to the UK. It cost them a fortune, but they said it was part of their tribute to the 2nd Air Division. Sadly this meant that we missed the big Duxford Show. However, we did get the crew and our PX stores up to Duxford by road, so at least we showed our faces and did a roaring trade in souvenirs. We were also invited to the special dinner in the

The crew with Norfolk Vintage Pilots at the Muckleburgh Collection, with Berry Savory second from left in back row.

The crew visit Liberator Close at Rackheath and the new 'Diamond Lil' house of R.J.Hastings Transport, with Roger Hastings at far right.

Officers' Mess at Duxford and were presented to His Royal Highness Prince Andrew.

Another great memory of the Tour was when Sir John Kemball invited the crew to spend some time with him at the Headquarters of Strike Command at RAF High Wycombe. This happened while the aircraft was still grounded at Biggin Hill so Jean and I drove my car and the crew bus down to collect them. The Air Vice Marshall made them very welcome and they enjoyed a tour of this famous wartime headquarters, including the room occupied by Air Chief Marshall 'Bomber' Harris. Then Kip announced a change of plan. Instead of dining in the Officers' Mess, he and Lady Kemball would entertain us in their home, Merton House – wonderful. Our two girl Colonels had never met a 'Lady' before and were worried as to how to address her. I told them to call her 'Ma'am' at first and that she would then tell them what to do. As I thought, when Starr first called her 'Ma'am', back came the response, 'Please call me Val.' Kip and Val Kemball gave us a truly memorable evening which the American crew never forgot. Kip had saved the project in so many ways – we can never thank him enough.

The wonderful evening at Merton House with Sir John and Lady Kemball. l. to r. Al Stricklin, Sir John, Lady Kemball, David Kjell, Ray Krottinger, Sam Mangrum, Starr Stone, Henry Brand.

During this time, Al Dexter and his wife Pat visited his old airfield at Hethel where he attempted to lift me over the hedge as he had done in 1943. On that occasion, having heard that I wanted to see his aeroplane, he rescued me from the airfield police, put an arm round my shoulder and walked me all round the aircraft and introduced me to the crew. More than that, he told me to 'come back anytime'. It was the beginning of a lifetime friendship. So now we revisited the old Base Chapel and the Control Tower and then enjoyed lunch at his favourite wartime pub the Bird in Hand. We were featured in an article in *Saga* magazine. They also enjoyed a day with the Jaguar Squadrons at Coltishall (including sitting in the cockpit) and were finally guests of honour at a Ladies Dining-in night at RAF Coltishall thanks to the kindness of Group Captain Phil Dacre, the Station Commander. This meant hiring a full black tie outfit for Al from a shop in Norwich, which was to cause huge laughs. They had never been to a formal RAF Dining-in night and it was a joy to watch their faces. Today's young

**The wartime B-24 Pilot at the RAF Coltishall Dining-in Night
l. to r. The author, Grp Capt. Phil Dacre, Jean Hastings, Pat Dexter, Lt Al Dexter, PMC**

RAF pilots were deeply impressed to have in their midst an American wartime bomber pilot who had completed 35 missions over Germany and they listened in awe to his brief address. Before they left Coltishall Al and Pat saw the famous painting 'Welcome Home Yank' (now at

The cover of the *Saga* magazine featuring Al Dexter's exploits and the renewal of his friendship with the author. Published September 1992.

Courtesy Saga Magazine

Radar Museum, RAF Neatishead) as well as the historic 'Battle of Britain Lace' (now in Norwich Cathedral). How sad it is that this famous Battle of Britain station, where we had been honorary members since 1968, has been closed.

The Thirty Mission Certificate presented to Lt Al Dexter in 1944.

Chapter 10

THE FLIGHT HOME

In early July 'Diamond Lil' finally arrived back at Norwich Airport for a few more days before she began the long haul back to Fort Worth. Once again we were inundated with visitors and did a few more local flights. Another CAF Colonel was flying over from the States to take my place so I realised with sadness that my times of flying 'Diamond Lil' were coming to an end.

We had a memorable 'Farewell Dinner' at Norwich Sports Village and were delighted that Connie, the charming wife of David Hughes, had joined the crew. Then, suddenly, David Hughes told Jean that I was to start packing when I got home as the pilot who was to replace me on the Trans-Atlantic crossing had not arrived. I could not believe my luck and just hoped that Bill Samuels and NorthWest would somehow get me back to the UK. David had planned for a 1430hrs departure from Norwich Airport, so I arrived after lunch and had to fight my way through the crowds that were waiting to see their favourite aircraft depart. We dumped all our kit in the bomb bay, did all the pre-flight checks including the props and then received a call from the Tower asking if we could accept a coach-load of visitors who were imploring the Airport for one last look. David agreed as long as it could be quick; little did we know what would be the result of our kindness. We showed them around the inside of the B-24, including the cockpit, and then they were gone.

Engines started and, with tears in our eyes, we taxied away to the holding point for runway 09 ready for our two-hour flight to Prestwick, where we had promised a brief display before landing. To the cheers and waves of the huge crowd on the Cromer Road, we took off. The Tower asked for another fly-past before we set course on a perfect day for flying. We climbed slowly up to 9,000ft under a military Radar clearance and then relaxed to the wonderful sound of the four Pratt & Whitneys. I enjoyed my last time at the controls and then, all too soon, we were in the descent to Prestwick, where David gave them a tremendous fifteen-minute display. We landed and were parked outside what appeared to be a disused cargo terminal and started to unload our kit. Al Stricklin had been in charge of the official CAF video camera and had been filming ever since the project began in April. He had kept the camera and all the tapes in a special case which he dumped in the bomb bay with all his other kit at Norwich. Al now asked who had got the case and, when no one answered, we searched the aircraft from nose to tail without success. We then realised that one of that last group of visitors, just prior to take-off, must have stolen the case. We were all shattered, especially me as it was my home airport. Later we informed the police but, despite radio and TV appeals, it was never returned. We had hoped that when the person responsible found that the camera and tapes were all in the American NTSC format he might have returned our historic films, but no such luck.

The Crew Change Arrives

The next day was spent checking 'Diamond Lil', route planning, and talking to Iqaluit in Canada. They told us that the tanker had still not got through the ice and that we had taken most of their Avgas on the way out so we would have to go slightly south to Goose Bay. Our two girl Colonels, Starr and Kathy, were delighted that they were going to be allowed to fly the Atlantic. Henry Brand found one of the carburettors was damp, so we arranged with our hotel to dry it out in one of their ovens – and it worked. Just as we arrived back at our hotel at the end of the day my replacement pilot walked in, full of apologies for having been delayed. Ray Krottinger, bless him, suggested that I could stay on for the flight, but Jean phoned to say that she was having a problem with Norwich Airport and I knew that I really could not spend any more time away from my business. So I sadly made the decision to return to Norwich by train the next day.

I had a wonderful dinner with the crew and knew that I was going to miss them tremendously, but we vowed to keep in touch and would meet again in the autumn when Jean and I attended the 2nd Air Division Annual Convention at Las Vegas.

So, with a very heavy heart, I shook hands with all the crew after breakfast, wished them a safe flight home and, still wearing my flight overalls, took the train to Glasgow. The long journey home was via Peterborough and it was amazing how many people wanted to talk to me when they saw my 'Diamond Lil' flight badge, especially when we got nearer to East Anglia. Jean, bless her, was waiting on the platform at Norwich for this very tired old pilot. For both of us it was the end of a tremendous experience with a great aeroplane and a superb crew. We had just been so lucky.

Shoulder patches worn by the 'Diamond Lil' crew.

Chapter 11

A PILOT'S THOUGHTS

As I look back through my Log Book it does not seem possible that I flew over 5,600 miles in a great B-24 Liberator and became a Colonel in the Confederate Air Force. What a joy it was that Jean was also made a Colonel in view of all her efforts on the ground; the crew were delighted to tell her that her service number was senior to mine.

I first have to thank Lt Al Dexter and the 389th at Hethel for making me so welcome and allowing me so many hours inside his B-24, 'Pugnacious Princess Pat', in 1944. My twenty-eight-year Governorship in the Memorial Trust of the 2nd Air Division enlarged my friendship with the United States and took me to that fortunate meeting with the Confederate Air Force at Harlingen in 1981. Finally came Tom Eaton's order for me to find a B-24 and bring it to England.

To fly with such an experienced and friendly crew, all qualified engineers as well as pilots was tremendous, and to have a senior Delta Airlines Captain as our Commander for the dangerous Arctic and Atlantic crossing was a great comfort. Then what can I say about my mentor, Ray Krottinger, who became such a good friend? I was delighted when, a few years later, he married one of our good-looking girl Scanners, Colonel Starr Stone, and we still chat regularly by email. I must not forget Alan Stricklin, who did all the arranging, or our Flight Engineers, David Kjell, Henry Brand and Sam Mangrum who taught me so much about 'round engines'. I will never forget David's gift in Iceland of his CAF belt buckle, which I still proudly wear today. I was just so fortunate to fly with such wonderful friends on such an awe-inspiring, once in a lifetime journey.

Then there were hundreds of people who helped to make the project so successful: Sir John Kemball and his wife Val, Bill Samuels and all the NorthWest team, who really spoilt me, the US Navy, 120 Squadron at RAF Kinloss, Group Captain Phil Dacre and all the Station at Coltishall, Group Captain George Keith, the Sport Village Team, Marion Stegeman Hodgson, Geoff and Terry Gregory, Jordan Uttal and the 2nd Air Division Association as well as all our sponsors. I must not forget the members of the Norwich Aviation Group who looked after 'Diamond Lil' so well during our stay at Norwich. We met so many wonderful people that it would be impossible to mention them all, but THANK YOU.

'Diamond Lil' was a great aircraft to fly, heavy as you would expect, but very sensitive in fore and aft trim. When you needed to turn she would think about it before she rolled, but there was no hesitation if you wanted to raise or lower the nose. It was amazing how those young American airmen flew tight formations at max weight during the war and flying the 'Lil' made you admire them even more. The castoring nose wheel could be exciting, but David Hughes and Ray Krottinger always demonstrated just how perfect a landing should be. Like all B-24s, there was always a strong smell of gasoline in the bomb bay. Watching the crew complete an engine change in just thirty-two hours at Keflavik was another lasting memory, but Simon Bates is best forgotten.

To watch the faces of all those whom we flew and see their tremendous enjoyment was so good, as was the realisation that in 1992 we had paid a fitting tribute to the bravery, sacrifice and friendship of the 2nd Air Division USAAF. After coping with engine failure over the Arctic icecap and crossing Greenland and the Denmark Strait on three engines, we had brought a B-24 Liberator home and made thousands of people happy on both sides of the Atlantic.

Sadly, in recent years, Al and Pat Dexter, Henry Brand, David Kjell, Geoff Gregory and Jordan Uttal have all 'folded their wings' but we will never forget them. 'Diamond Lil' is still flying the air show circuit in the United States, but now under a new name 'Ole 927'.

Chapter 12

THE AFTERMATH

After 'Diamond Lil' had safely returned home via Goose Bay, work began on the Wide Screen Audio/Visual production entitled 'The Return of the Liberator', ready for a premiere in September at the Norwich Sport Village. When the film had been processed we had a unique record lasting 75 minutes in full colour with Hi-Fi sound on a 14ft-wide screen. We were given the superb Central Arena at the Sport

Village seating five hundred and NorthWest provided a colourful backdrop. A local artist, who had produced a superb painting of 'Diamond Lil' escorted by the three RAF Jaguars, asked if he could sell prints of the picture at the Premiere, to which we gladly agreed. We advertised in the local press and to our amazement we had to hold three Premieres before everyone was catered for. Tom Eaton introduced the film at each showing, the artist sold his prints well and we received a large donation towards the 2nd Air Division Memorial Library. The film went on tour throughout Norfolk to be enjoyed by packed audiences in village halls and, twenty years on, is still one of the most heavily booked films in our shows. At a show in North Walsham we noticed in the interval that an old man in the audience was very upset. Apparently, the sound of the Pratt & Whitneys over the Atlantic was too much for him; he was the co-pilot of the famous Squadron Leader Bullock and they held the record for the number of U-boat kills. We also gave talks about our epic journey, even going as far as Duxford.

It was obvious that, despite the tragic loss of the official CAF film at Norwich, we ought to try to produce a record from the other video cameras on board including mine. I managed to get all the film together and found a London film studio willing to produce the film and a local Silver Band kindly provided the background music. Once more the demand was amazing – we must have produced thousands much to the benefit of the Memorial Library.

In October 1992 Jean and I flew out to stay with Geoff and Terry Gregory at Dallas for a few days before they took us in their super van to the 2nd Air Division Annual Convention at Las Vegas, via Phoenix, the Grand Canyon, and Mount Sion National Park. Before we left Dallas we had a wonderful reunion with all the 'Diamond Lil' crew at Fort Worth (including the now traditional Margaritas). At the splendid Convention Banquet I had to address over 1800 veterans and their families and tell them about our epic flight to England in their memory, something I found far more frightening than the flight itself.

So there it is, and I hope you have enjoyed reading the memories of this very old retired pilot, who was so lucky in 1992 to be involved in a historic and never-to-be-repeated B-24 Liberator flight with such a tremendous crew.

APPENDIX 1

AIRCRAFT HISTORY AND SPECIFICATIONS
B-24A LIBERATOR AM927 'DIAMOND LIL'

Liberator AM927 was built by the Consolidated Aircraft Corporation at their San Diego factory in California in May 1941 and was number 18 out of a total of over 18,000 produced. Originally she was destined for the French Air Force, but after the fall of France she was allocated to the Royal Air Force and No. 120 Squadron. After a landing accident on her delivery flight she was returned to the factory and converted to a transport version with the name of 'Old 927'. She flew in this category throughout the war on a regular scheduled basis between San Diego, Fort Worth, New York and Washington DC. She was also used as the personal transport for Madame Chiang Kai-Shek during her visit to the USA.

After the war she was sold to the Continental Can Company, refurbished and flown as an Executive aircraft for ten years before being sold to Petroleus Mexicanos (PEMEX). In 1971 the aircraft was purchased by the Confederate Air Force, named 'Diamond Lil' and repainted in the colours and markings of the 98th Bomb Group, 'The Pyramiders' of the 9th US Army Air Force. In 2010 she was renamed 'Ole 927' and still flies as part of the B-29/B-24 Squadron of the Commemorative Air Force at Fort Worth, Texas.

Wingspan	110ft
Length	66ft 4ins
Engines	Four Pratt & Whitney 1830-94 Radial
Gross Weight	58,000lbs
Fuel Capacity	3,000 gallons
Fuel Consumption	200 gallons per hour
Oil Capacity	35 gallons each engine
Cruise Speed	200mph

The cockpit and instrument panel of 'Diamond Lil' from the right seat.

The nose art on 'Diamond Lil'.

APPENDIX 2

CERTIFICATES AND MEMORABILIA

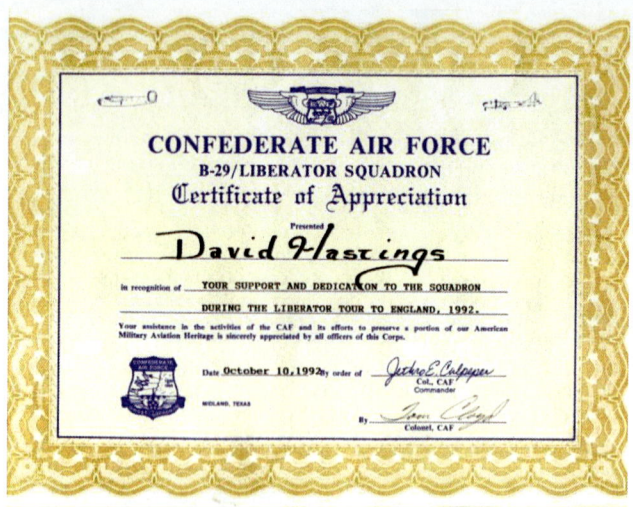

Confederate Air Force Certificate, October 1992.

Commissioning warrant as Colonel in the CAF 1992.

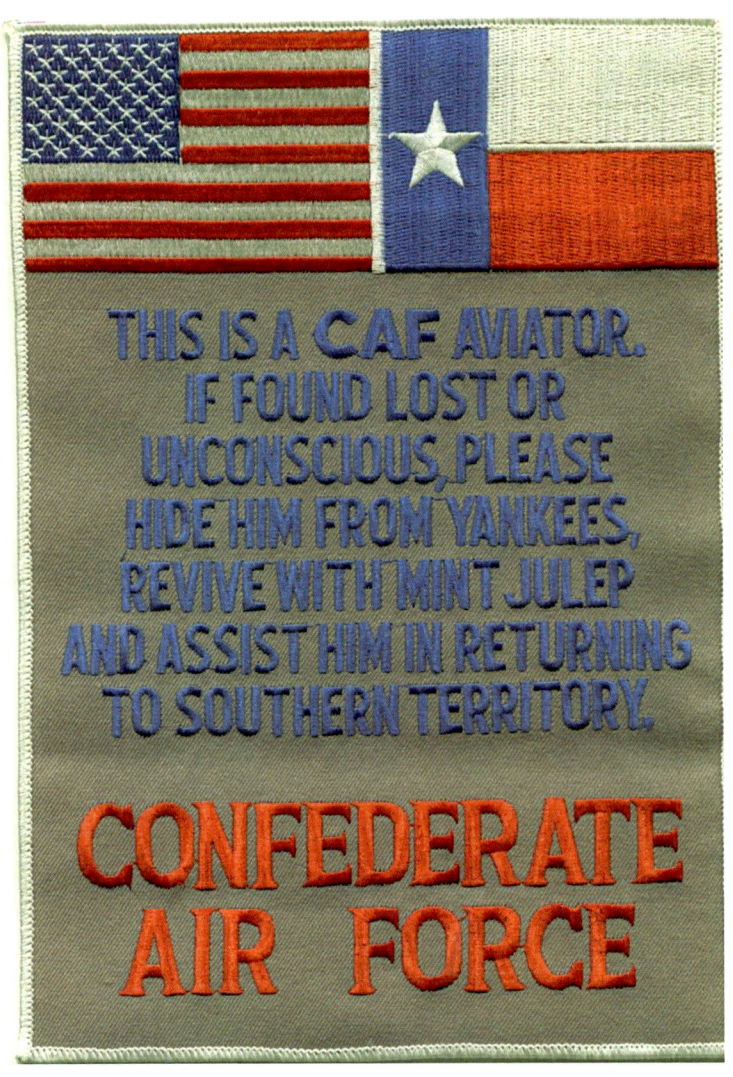

The back patch worn by the Confederate Air Force crew in case of emergency.

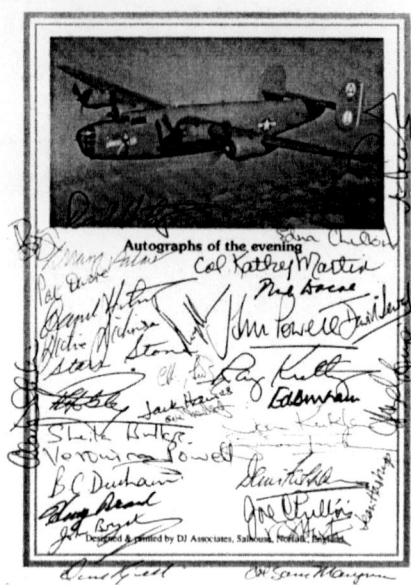
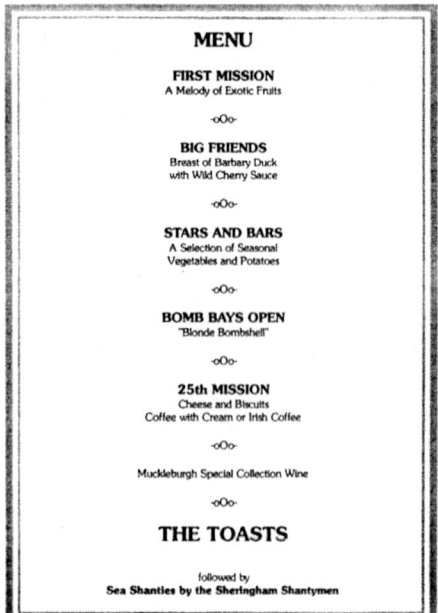

The souvenir menu with the crew signatures after the Norfolk Vintage Pilots' Dinner at Muckleburgh.

WE THANK YOU

THE MAIN SPONSORS

NORTHWEST AIRLINES

NORWICH SPORT VILLAGE & HOTEL in Broadland

Pelham
PELHAM HOMES NORFOLK LIMITED

HOTEL NORWICH

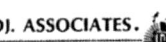 

AirUK engineering

Eastern Stearman

The Memorial Trust of the 2nd Air Division U.S.A.A.F.

In addition we have received many individual donations to support this unique flight across the Atlantic in this special USAAF 50th Anniversary Year. Help is still needed, please see the Crew if you are willing to support the project. The Confederate Air Force and the Memorial Trust of the 2nd Air Division USAAF would like to thank most sincerely all the sponsors, large and small who have helped to make this dream come true so that once again the UK can see and hear the roar of a Liberator.

"They came as Friends, They stayed as Friends and they have remained Friends"

Printed and designed by DJ Associates, Salhouse, Norfolk, England.

The cover of the East Anglian Tourist Board brochure and the B-24 type tag for AM927.

THE CREW'S LAMENT

I am the Captain, I sit on the left,
I'm very skilful and terribly deft.
I suffer in silence while Joe on my right
Makes all his circuits a little too tight.
I never go crook when he drops too much flap,
I like his sweet smile as he says 'sorry Cap',
Then bashes the trim with a twist and a twirl,
As he raves of the virtues and curves of his girl.
I select cruising power and call for coarse pitch,
Joe grabs the mixtures and slams them full pitch,
When it's time to change tanks Joe turns the wrong tap,
When I call for 'gear up' he drops ten degrees flap.
He's late for take-off first flight of each morning,
I do the run-up while Joe does the yawning.
He's never quite sure of his check points or courses,
I fake the log while Joe swots up the horses.
When I give him a landing he gives me the pip,
As the Tower calls up and says 'Stay on the Strip',
'Ignorant type' says Joe on my right,
Then dates up the hostess for Saturday night.
When the ceiling's right down and I fly on the gauges,
Joe says a prayer and then chants 'Rock of Ages'.
I envy the guy who said God is my Co,
Oh, what I'd give to swap him for Joe.

I am the Co-pilot, I sit on the right,
It's up to me to be quick and be bright.
I never talk back for I have no regrets,
But I have to remember what the Captain forgets.
I make out the flight plan and study the weather,
Pull up the gear and stand by to feather,
Make out the mail form and do the reporting,
And fly the old crate while the Captain is snoring.
I take all the readings and adjust the power,
Put on the heaters when we enter a shower,
Tell where we are on the darkest of night,
And do all the bookwork without any light.
I call for the Captain and buy him Cokes,
I always laugh at his corny jokes,
And once in a while, when his landings are rusty,
I always come through with 'by gosh, but it's gusty'.
All in all I'm a general stooge,
As I sit on the right of a man they call Scrooge.
I guess you think that it's past understanding,
But maybe someday he'll give me a landing.

**The end of the journey.
A British 'schoolboy' and an American wartime pilot are united once again at Norwich International Airport in June 1992.
l. to r. The author, Col. David Hastings, and Lt Al Dexter 389th BG 2nd Air Division USAAF**

Courtesy Archant – Eastern Daily Press